9/00

D0548849

Born to be Wild
Little Whales

Violette Rennert

Words that appear in the glossary are printed in
boldface type the first time they occur in the text.

GARETH**STEVENS**
PUBLISHING
A Member of the WRC Media Family of Companies

Living in the Sea

Snuggled close against its mother's huge side, a baby whale, or calf, is not afraid of anything. The mother whale's rich, warm milk flows out of her body and directly into her calf's throat. Blue water is all around them — they are in the sea. From time to time, they swim up to the surface of the water to breathe, then dive underwater to feed again. The mother whale always looks after her calf. If the calf swims too far from her side, she punishes it by hitting it with her **fin**. Away from its mother, a little whale would be in danger if killer whales or sharks were close by.

A female whale, called a cow, gives birth to only one calf at a time. At birth, the calf already weighs between 1 and 6 tons (1 and 5 tonnes) — almost as much as an adult elephant!

What do you think?

Why do whales blow out water through their **blowholes**?

a) so they can take a breath

b) so they can make bubbles and have fun

c) so they can send signals to other whales

Whales blow out water through their blowholes so they can take a breath.

Even though baby whales look like giant fish, they are **mammals**. They are warm-blooded, drink their mothers' milk, and have **lungs** for breathing. A whale can stay underwater for a long time, but it must swim to the surface regularly for air to breathe. At the surface, it blows out very strongly through its blowholes, spitting out everything it has in its lungs and producing a huge jet of water that can be seen from far away. Then the whale takes a deep breath, filling its lungs with air before diving underwater again.

A whale's nostrils, or blowholes, are little holes located on the top of its head. They close when the whale's head is underwater so the whale will not breathe water into its lungs.

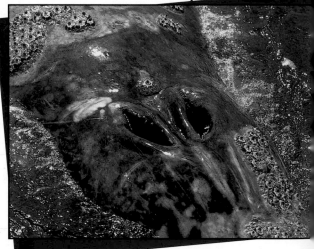

Humans can tell whales apart by the way they blow water through their blowholes. Each kind of whale does it a different way. Blue whales can produce jets of water up to 40 feet (12 meters) high.

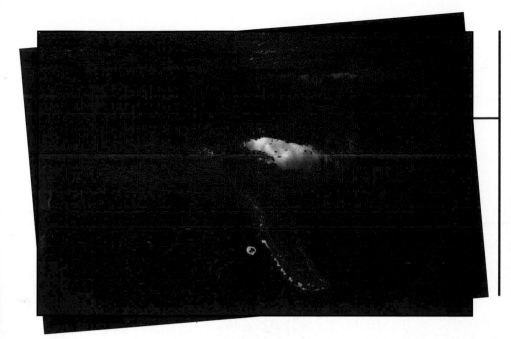

Over millions of years, the bodies of whales have changed to allow them to live in water. Their front legs became flippers. Their back legs turned into one large tail formed by two fins called **flukes**.

Like sharks and dolphins, many kinds of whales, including humpback whales, have a **dorsal fin** on their backs.

Off to the Poles

By springtime, young whale calves have grown a lot. They are ready to swim from the warm waters where they were born to the cold seas near the North and South Poles. A calf makes this **migration** with its mother and a few other whales. The trip is long, sometimes more than 12,000 miles (19,300 kilometers), and it will last three months. The whales swim day and night near the surface of the water, making only quick stops to sleep.

What do you think?

Why do whales migrate every year?

a) because they like to travel

b) because they are curious about new places

c) because they like to be cool during summer and warm in winter

Despite its huge size, a whale is a very good swimmer. It **propels** itself through the water with its big tail and can reach speeds of up to 30 miles (48 km) an hour — the speed of a car on a city street.

Whales migrate because they like to be cool during summer and warm in winter.

The oceans around the North and South Poles are ice cold, but this is where whales find their favorite food — tiny shrimp called krill. Each summer, whales eat tons of krill. As soon as winter comes, however, and the waters at the Poles start to freeze, the whales swim to **tropical** areas. There, the air is never cold, the water is warm, and the ocean is not too deep. Food is hard to find in tropical seas, but they are much better places to **mate** and give birth to baby whales.

Whales' favorite places to mate are the waters of **Oceania**, Africa, and South America. But when warmer weather returns to the Poles, most whales swim back to the Arctic or Antarctic Oceans.

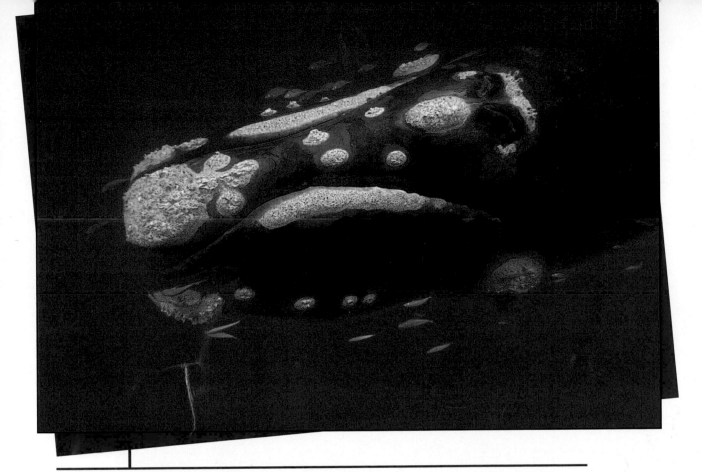

A whale is never alone, even when it travels. About 600 to 1,100 pounds (275 to 500 kilograms) of small sea animals called **barnacles** spend their lives clinging to a whale's body. Fortunately, barnacles do not bother or harm whales.

Whales do not like crowds. They usually travel in small groups, with only two to six whales in a group.

Big Appetites

In its second year, a whale calf swims with its mother to look for large groups, or schools, of krill. Searching for and eating krill take up most of their time. Whales need a lot of food to build up a thick layer of fat all over their bodies. The fat helps keep the whales warm in cold waters and will be a reserve of food for them during winter. A whale's layer of fat also acts like an inner tube, keeping the whale floating on the surface of the water when it sleeps.

A female whale feeds her calf milk for about one year. At a rate of 130 gallons (490 liters) of milk a day, a mother whale can lose up to 55 tons (50 tonnes), or half, of her body weight in that year.

What do you think?

How does a whale find food?

a) It swims with its mouth open.

b) It follows dolphins or sharks that are hunting for food.

c) It hides and waits for fish to swim past it.

Whales swallow their food without chewing it. Whales that have teeth use them only to catch or tear their food. Many kinds of whales do not have teeth. These whales have baleen plates, which are long, thin strings of flexible, hornlike material that form a kind of net hanging from the whales' upper jaws. To eat, a whale opens its mouth very wide, scooping up everything it can. Then, the whale pushes the water out of its mouth with its giant tongue, and the baleen plates trap thousands of little fish. The whale immediately swallows the fish whole. A whale does not need to chew its food because its stomach can **digest** everything.

Humpback whales have a strange way of hunting. Using their blowholes, they blow circles of air bubbles around schools of krill, trapping them. The krill gather in tight groups in the middle of the circles. Then the whales just open their mouths wide and gobble up their dinner.

Because of its baleen plates, a whale can swallow only little fish and small sea animals. But a whale makes up for its limited diet by eating at least 1,100 pounds (500 kg) of food a day! Seagulls often snatch the fish that escape from a whale's mouth.

Baleen plates can measure more than 10 feet (3 m) long, and a whale can have up to eight thousand of them. A whale's tongue can weigh as much as an adult elephant!

What a Life!

Whales seem to have lots of fun. They jump out of the water and land flat on their stomachs or backs, making loud noises and huge splashes when they hit the water. Sometimes, they make noise by forcefully slapping their tails on the surface of the water. This noise often sounds like a drum. A whale can slide, dive, turn somersaults, or bounce in any direction. When having fun has made a little whale tired, it swims onto the soft, smooth skin of its mother's slippery back to rest.

What do you think?

How do whales communicate with each other?

a) They perform dances for each other.

b) They sing to each other.

c) They clap their fins to pass along messages.

Whales use their fins to steer, stop, and make big movements. Compared to the length of their bodies, humpback whales have longer **pectoral fins** than any other kinds of whales.

Whales communicate by singing to each other.

When humans are near the ocean, they sometimes can hear strange moans coming from far away. These sounds are the "songs" of whales. The songs sound like babbling and can last for several hours or days. "Singing" is how whales communicate with each other. When whales gather during the winter mating season, male whales sing songs or make other sounds to attract female whales.

Each whale group has its own songs. Humpback whales sing songs that can last thirty minutes, and they will repeat them for hours. The humpbacks' songs also change a little from one year to the next.

Whales have tiny ears, but they can still hear sounds from far away. The ears of some kinds of whales have wax inside them to keep water out.

Whales have a strong sense of touch. Their skin is very sensitive, and bumps around their mouths contain hairs that look and act like whiskers, helping the whale feel what is around it.

New Adventures

After two years, a young whale is old enough to leave its mother. It knows the routes of the seasonal migrations, the songs of the adults, the places to find large groups of krill, and where to stay warm. It has also learned how to avoid the ocean's dangers. The young whale is ready to go off by itself or join another small group of whales. It will have to wait until it is about fifteen years old, however, before it is able to mate.

A whale is a diving champion. It can dive to about 1,150 feet (350 m) and stay underwater for up to fifty minutes.

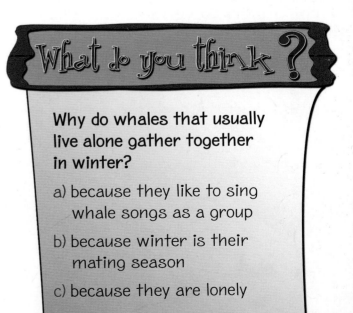

What do you think?

Why do whales that usually live alone gather together in winter?

a) because they like to sing whale songs as a group

b) because winter is their mating season

c) because they are lonely

During winter, whales gather in warm, tropical waters to mate. The males swim around the females, singing to them for days. When mating season is over, the males leave the females and live on their own or with other males. Females carry their babies for ten to twelve months and give birth the following winter. Other female whales help mother whales give birth by protecting them from sharks and by helping newborn calves swim to the surface of the water to breathe.

To attract females, male whales fight, blow water out of their blowholes, and jump high out of the water. They put on quite a show!

Male humpback whales use their fins to jump and show their strength. Only the strongest male in a group will mate with the female that is nearby.

Winter is the time for whale songs and parades of male whales
jumping out of the water as they try to attract females for mating.

Whales are marine mammals, which means they live in water. They mainly live in tropical and polar regions but can be found in any sea on Earth. A whale can live from eighty to one hundred years. Adult whales weigh between 27 and 155 tons (25 and 140 tonnes), depending on the kind of whale. Blue whales are the largest animals on Earth. They can weigh more than 100 tons (90 tonnes) and measure 100 feet (30 m) long.

There are about eighty kinds of whales. All whales are related to dolphins and porpoises.

From their heads to their tails, whales are between 25 and 100 feet (8 and 30 m) long — the length of one to three buses placed end to end.

Whales use their side, or pectoral, fins to steer. These fins can be rounded or pointed and can measure 10 to 20 feet (3 to 6 m) long.

A whale uses its blowholes to breathe air. A baleen whale, such as a humpback or a blue whale, has two blowholes. A whale with teeth, such as a killer whale, has only one blowhole.

The hairs around a whale's mouth act like whiskers and are as sensitive as a cat's whiskers. The whale uses these hairs to feel what is in front of it.

A whale's ears are small holes that are hidden behind the whale's eyes.

A whale's small eyes are on opposite sides of its head. Whales can see both under and above the water.

GLOSSARY

barnacles — small, hard-shelled sea animals that cling to whales, rocks, and the bottoms of boats

blowholes — the breathing holes on the tops of the heads of some marine mammals

digest — to break down food into a form that can be absorbed and used by the body

dorsal fin — the fin on the backs of some water animals

fin — one of the thin, flat parts that stick out of the bodies of whales and other marine animals

flukes — the two halves of a whale's tail

lungs — the body organs used by humans and many other animals for breathing air

mammals — warm-blooded animals that have backbones, give birth to live babies, feed their young with milk from the mother's body, and have skin that is usually covered with hair or fur

mate — (v) to join together to produce young

migration — a journey from one place or climate to another

Oceania — the lands in the central and south Pacific Ocean

pectoral fins — fins that are located where front legs would be

propels — moves forward with a forceful motion

tropical — of or related to the warmest regions of Earth

Please visit our web site at: **www.garethstevens.com**
For a free color catalog describing Gareth Stevens Publishing's list of high-quality books and multimedia programs, call 1-800-542-2595 (USA) or 1-800-387-3178 (Canada). Gareth Stevens Publishing's fax: (414) 332-3567.

Library of Congress Cataloging-in-Publication Data

Rennert, Violette.
  [Petite baleine. English]
  Little whales / Violette Rennert. — North American ed.
    p. cm. — (Born to be wild)
  ISBN 0-8368-4740-7 (lib. bdg.)
  1. Humpback whale—Infancy—Juvenile literature. I. Title. II. Series.
QL737.C424R4713   2005
599.5'139—dc22   2004065372

This North American edition first published in 2006 by
Gareth Stevens Publishing
A Member of the WRC Media Family of Companies
330 West Olive Street, Suite 100
Milwaukee, Wisconsin 53212 USA

This U.S. edition copyright © 2006 by Gareth Stevens, Inc.
Original edition copyright © 2001 by Mango Jeunesse.

First published in 2001 as *La petite baleine* by Mango Jeunesse, an imprint of Editions Mango, Paris, France.

Picture Credits (t=top, b=bottom, l=left, r=right)
Bios: G. Martin 5(b); J. M Bour 9(b), 12; L. Cogniet/P. Arnol 13(t); Y. Lefevre 18; J. Watt/Panda photo 20(t), 22. Jacana: Y. Gladu 2; S. Cordier 6, 15. PHONE: F. Gohier 4(t), 13(b), 14, 17(t), 21, 22–23; J. P. Ferrero 16. Sunset: Animals animals title page, 7, back cover; Brake 4(b), 20(b); V. Audet cover, 5(t); G. Lacz 8, 17(b); Ant 9(t); J. Warden cover; D. Perrine 10.

English translation: Muriel Castille
Gareth Stevens editor: Barbara Kiely Miller
Gareth Stevens art direction: Tammy West
Gareth Stevens designer: Jenni Gaylord

All rights reserved. No part of this book may be reproduced, stored in a retrieval system, or transmitted in any form or by any means, electronic, mechanical, photocopying, recording, or otherwise, without the prior written permission of the copyright holder.

Printed in the United States of America

1 2 3 4 5 6 7 8 9 09 08 07 06 05